TRAINING

Bible
Activities
and Object
Lessons
for Families
with
Preschoolers

Wiggles, Giggles, & Popcorn

KIRK WEAVER

To Jim Weidmann, who introduced me to the priceless joy and peace that comes from providing intentional spiritual training in the home. To my family—Kelly, Madison, and McKinley—who have embraced Family Time as a core value in our life together. And, to our unborn grandchildren and great-grandchildren, may you learn, live, and teach Jesus as our personal Savior and eternal hope.

To Pat and Sharon Winn, who from the very beginning embraced the challenge of helping our family follow God's leading in the establishment of Family Time Training. Silently and without question, they have encouraged and provided a strong foundation on which to stand as we stepped out into the unknown. God is using Pat and Sharon to reach the next generation with the Good News of Jesus Christ.

—Kirk Weaver

Table of Contents

Family Activities

Teaching Goal: Noah obeyed God when he built the ark.
Scripture: Genesis 6:14-16

Teaching Goal: God protected baby Moses.
Scripture: Exodus 2:3

Teaching Goal: Family relationships are special.
Scripture: Book of Ruth

Teaching Goal: Showing hospitality is a privilege.
Scripture: Acts 18:1-2, 1 Corinthians 16:19, 1 Peter 4:9

Teaching Goal: When we fill our lives with the teachings of Jesus
then we will bear the fruit of the Spirit.
Scripture: Psalm 1:2-3, Galatians 5:22-23

Teaching Goal: We need to keep growing spiritually throughout
our lives.
Scripture: Philippians 1:6, 1 Peter 2:2

Teaching Goal: God lives in heaven.
Scripture: Deuteronomy 26:15

Teaching Goal: Jesus went to heaven to prepare a place for us.
Scripture: John 14:2-4

Mission

The mission of Family Time Training is to reach future generations with the Good News of Christ by training parents to teach their children Christian principles, values, and beliefs in the home.

Vision Statement

Imagine a child who responds to the needs of others and is eager to give and share.

Imagine a child who has learned to say "no" to busyness. A child who will take time to slow down and who understands the necessity of Sabbath rest.

Imagine a child who has been trained to seek truth.

Imagine a child who lives accountable to an unseen but always present God.

Imagine a child whose best friend is Jesus.

Imagine a child who is more eager to learn about the teachings of Jesus than to watch television or play sports.

Imagine a child with an eternal perspective, a child who invests more time giving and serving than accumulating and being entertained.

Imagine hundreds and thousands, a whole generation, of children growing up to live and teach the example of Christ.

In Deuteronomy 6:7 God presents his plan for passing on a godly heritage to our children. At Family Time Training our vision is to see future generations living for Christ. First, parents are to be the primary spiritual teachers in the lives of children. Second, spiritual training is to take place 24 hours a day, seven days a week. Family Time Training is just a tool, but it is a tool God can use in your family to accomplish his vision.

Foreword

"I believe most parents who are Christian want to teach their children the faith, they just don't know how. The church is important support but primary spiritual teaching must happen in the home, otherwise, it's not going to happen."

—R.C. Sproul, theologian

Family Time is the "how to" tool parents can use to teach their children the faith at home. The organization Family Time Training equips parents with fun and exciting activities designed to teach children Christian principles, values, and beliefs.

Family Time Training was formed in response to a spiritual crisis that threatens to undermine the foundation of today's families. For generations, Christian parents have abdicated to the church their God-given role as the primary spiritual leaders for their children. The church is expected to build within the lives of children a strong spiritual foundation in just one or two hours per week. God designed spiritual training to take place 24 hours a day, seven days a week, with the parents providing primary leadership and the church providing important support. For the sake of our children we must return proactive spiritual training to the home.

Family Time Training works with churches, schools, and spiritually-based groups to teach parents how to provide home-based spiritual training. Training is provided through sermons, classes, and weekend seminars. Families receive direct support through a website (www.famtime.com), activity books, and quarterly mailings.

—Kirk Weaver

Introduction

Not long ago, my wife Kelly and I were talking with Madison on her bed in her room. She was upset with the kids at school. Some were picking on an unpopular student, playing a cruel game Madi chose not to play, and it left her separated from her girlfriends. With tears flowing down her face, Madi said, "I'm trying to be like the beans in Dad's story."

Madi was referring to a Family Time lesson. The activity is built around three pots of boiling water, with the water representing adversity. We drop a carrot into the first pot, an egg into the second, and coffee beans into the third. What choices will we make in response to the adversity we face in our lives? Do we get soft like the carrot the way Peter did when he denied Christ? Does the adversity make us hard like the egg and Pharaoh's heart? Or like the coffee beans, which can represent the example of Paul, do we influence and change the environment around us? Madi was applying a lesson that we'd taught more than four months earlier.

As a parent, you've had moments like this. You know what they're worth.

Family Time activities are simple, fun object lessons intended to teach children about life in God's world. This is a book of ideas for structured teaching times that will carry forward and open doors for informal learning moments. At first it may feel a little clumsy to create the structured time, to boil carrots and eggs and coffee beans. But the moments when your child actively chooses the godly path will fuel your love and your relationship like nothing else in the world.

"Here's the game," I told the four children, my son, daughter, and two neighborhood friends. They were standing at the bottom of the stairs, wide-eyed and eager for the Family Time activity. Standing at the top of the stairs, I said, "I represent Jesus in heaven. More than anything I want you up here with me, but, you can't use the stairs and you can't use the handrails."

They knew there was a trick, something to learn. But what? How would they get from the bottom of the stairs to the top without touching the stairs or the railing? My daughter ran to get a laundry basket, turned it upside down, stood on top and reached up only to find she was still more than fifteen steps from the top.

It was my son, Mac, the youngest of the four, who figured out the solution. "I got it! Dad, please come down and get me," his face beaming, because he had solved the riddle. I descended the stairs.

"Will you carry me to the top?" he asked. "Of course!" I responded. After carrying all four children piggyback style to the second floor, I said, "That's how you get to heaven. You can't do it on your own. Only through Jesus can you get there." A powerful lesson presented in the language of children that they still remember to this day.

Deuteronomy 6:5-9 says:
"Love the LORD your God with all your heart and with all your soul and with all your strength. These commandments that I give you today are to be upon your hearts. Impress them on your children."

How?
"Talk about them when you sit at home and when you walk along the road, when you lie down and when you get up. Tie them as symbols on your hands and bind them on your foreheads. Write them on the doorframes of your houses and on your gates."

How will we shape our children? What mark will we leave upon them? Is it possible that we can launch them into the world stronger, purer, more trusting of God than we were? Is it possible that we can reshape our families and our family interactions around the joy of loving God with all that is within us?

I believe it is possible. That's what this book is for.

The ABC's of Effective Family Times

A **Attention Span:** The rule of thumb for attention span is one minute for each year of age. A three-year-old may have a three-minute attention span. Break up your Family Time into three-minute increments. With variety, you gain additional attention span. For example:

3 minutes	Sing or play your Family Time theme song
2 minutes	Pray
3 minutes	Tell the story
3 minutes	Demonstrate the object lesson
3 minutes	Let the child repeat the object lesson
3 minutes	Retell the story
2 minutes	Practice memorization
2 minutes	Close in prayer

21 minutes	Total Family Time

B **Be Prepared to Say "I Don't Know":** Your children WILL ask you a question that you cannot answer. Promise to find the answer and get back to them within 24 hours. You can call a pastor or search the Internet for more information.

C **Call it Family Time:** When your children grow up you want them to have fond, lasting memories of Family Time. When referring to your times of formal spiritual training, say "Family Time" often. In the same way your children will remember going to school and church or playing sports and music, they will remember times of spiritual training called "Family Time."

D **Drama Queens and Kings:** Kids love to put on plays. Pick a Bible Story, assign the roles from Director to Diva—everyone gets in on the act. Don't forget to assign a videographer so you can watch it later.

E Encourage Guessing: Answering a question involves risk. Your child's answer may be right or wrong. Praise him when he guesses at an answer. If he gives the wrong answer say, "Great guess! The answer is..." and give him the correct information. This will keep him participating. If you say, "No, that's wrong," children may eventually stop talking.

F Fixed or Flexible: It's great and admirable to have Family Time the same night every week. However, it may not be practical for your family. Be willing to move the night if needed. The important thing is to have at least one Family Time each week.

G Give it to God: God commands parents and grandparents to be spiritual teachers with their children (Deuteronomy 6:7; Deuteronomy 4:9, Psalm 78:5). Trust that God will equip you to fulfill his plan. As you prepare, and before you begin your Family Time each week, pray and ask the Holy Spirit to lead you and clearly communicate the message to your children.

H Hold the Distractions: When sitting at the table, remove the centerpiece, pencils, paper...anything that can distract a child. A random paper clip left on a table can lead to a possession battle that will ruin the atmosphere for Family Time. Also, when using materials like balloons, string, etc., don't bring them out until you're ready to use them.

I Involve Kids in the Preparations: Whenever possible, especially as kids get a little older, involve kids in the lesson preparations. Preparation can be as much fun as doing the activity and certainly increases ownership. Kids will enjoy making an obstacle course, building a tent with sheets, or mixing a big batch of cornstarch.

J Just Do It!: Don't wait another day to get started!

K Kitchen Table: Start your Family Time at the kitchen table even if you are only going to be there for a few minutes. Chairs provide natural boundaries that will help children focus as you explain what will happen during the Family Time.

L Listen to the Holy Spirit: Be prepared to modify or change the discussion if the Spirit moves the conversation in a different direction.

M Make a Picture: Coloring a picture to reinforce a Bible Story can be an excellent teaching technique. While the family is coloring, great conversation about the lesson can take place.

N Not a Spectator Sport: Participate with your children in the game or activity. By participating, you show your kids that you value Family Time.

O Oh Boy! If you're feeling frustrated or if family members have a negative attitude—reschedule. Keep it positive.

P Play it Again, Sam: For younger children, put the lesson into a one sentence phrase like: "Noah had faith in God." Or, "Be content with what God sent." The same night at bedtime, remind children of the main point. The following morning ask them what they remember from Family Time the night before.

Q Quitting isn't an Option: Commit to once a week and do your best not to take a week off. Continue to do Family Time during the summer months. If you stop, your kids will sense a lack of commitment to Family Time on your part.

R Repetition isn't the Same as Redundant: Younger children learn best through repetition. In the same way they will watch a video over and over, they may want to repeat fun Family Time activities. Be prepared to repeat the activity, asking the children to explain what the different elements represent. Consider repeating with neighborhood children; your children will learn even more when they teach others.

S Simple Structure: Younger children benefit from a structured time together. Consider following the Family Time Format each week.

T **To Be or Not to Be Silly:** Model for your children that it's okay to be dramatic, silly, and have fun. Kids love it when their parents are playful.

U **Unique Locations:** Have a church service in a crawl space to represent the early church under persecution. Hold your Family Time outside at a neighborhood park. Repeat fun activities when visiting relatives on vacation. Tell the story of Zacchaeus while sitting in a tree house. Changing the setting of your Family Time can be fun.

V **Variety:** Using a video clip can be an excellent way to teach a lesson. However, using video clips three weeks in a row becomes predictable and is less effective. Mix up the format and tools you use in your weekly Family Time (coloring, video clips, a snack tied to the lesson, etc.).

W **Watch Out for Unrealistic Expectations:** Family Time is seldom a disappointment to children. However, parents may sometimes feel like the lesson did not go as well as they had hoped. Often this disappointment is directly related to the parent's expectations. Keep in mind that kids learn valuable things over time. You don't have to get something fantastic out of each Family Time. Be prepared to learn right along with your kids.

X **Xpect a Future:** One day your children will grow up and start families of their own. As your children raise your grandchildren they will be equipped with positive memories and effective tools to pass along the faith of their fathers.

Y **Y? Y? Y?** Questions are cool. Frederick Beuchner says, "If you want big answers then ask small questions." "What did you learn at Sunday School?" is a big question. "Who did you sit next to at Sunday School?" is a smaller question that can lead to more discussion.

Z **Zees ees Fun!** Remember the most important things you can do: take your time, engage your child, and have fun together. A silly accent never hurts either!

Family Time Format

The "Family Time Format" is a simple structure that families can use when leading a Family Time activity. You may want to tweak and modify the structure to meet the needs of your family.

Younger children benefit from using the same format from week to week. They may want to repeat the activity again and again. Remember, repetition is how young children learn. Be sure to call your time together "Family Time." When your kids are grown, you want them to look back and be able to identify times of formal spiritual training in the same way they can identify school, sports, and church.

Families of older children may want to make the lesson less formal. For example, you may not have a "Family Time Theme Song." Instead, you can invite your teens to share a favorite song. Ask them why they like the song. Is it the beat, the singer, the words?

Meet Weekly:
The goal is to lead a weekly Family Time in your home. Try to designate and reserve the same time each week, recognizing that on occasion you will need the flexibility to schedule around conflicts.

No Fuss Dinner:
Plan a simple dinner so that everyone in the family can participate. You don't want one parent spending a lot of time fixing the meal and another parent spending a lot of time cleaning up. Minimize dinner preparation and clean-up by using paper plates and paper cups. Just by looking at how the table is set, children will know it's Family Time night. You may want to use leftovers or order in dinner. Keep it simple.

Discuss the Previous Family Time:
During dinner talk about what the family did last week during Family Time. Challenge the children to try and remember the activity and message. Talk about the

highlights and use this time to reinforce the message and its potential application during the past week.

You'll be surprised to learn that children will remember back two weeks, three weeks, maybe more.

Family Time Theme Song:

Pick your own family "theme song." Since this is for your spiritual training time, consider songs that talk about faith, family, relationships, and love.

Play this song after dinner and just before the evening lesson and activity. Younger children like to create a dance or hand motions to go with the song. This song signals that Family Time is here while building excitement and anticipation.

SONG IDEAS:
"The Family Prayer Song (As For Me and My House)" by Maranatha
"Creed" by Rich Mullins

Prayer:

Open the Family Time with prayer. Children and parents can take turns. Teach the children to pray about a wide variety of topics, joys, and concerns.

Message:

Decide in advance and practice the activity you will use. Communicate clearly the main principle or value being taught through the lesson.

Object Lesson:

Each Family Time has an object lesson or activity that reinforces and helps children remember the main message.

Memorize:

Repeat the short, rhyming phrase included with the lesson. The rhyme is designed to help children remember the lesson.

Prayer:

Close the time together with a prayer. Tie the prayer to the lesson. Try different methods of prayer such as holding hands and praying, pray from oldest to youngest, or say "popcorn" prayers (one- or two-word prayers about a specific topic).

Plan Ahead for Next Week:

Many lessons require that you gather specific objects or purchase items from the store. Look ahead to next week's Family Time activity to make sure you have all the necessary ingredients.

Lesson 1:
NOAH'S ARK

TEACHING GOAL: Noah obeyed God when he built the ark.

1. Play theme song
2. Pray
3. Lesson and discussion
4. Memorize: **People thought Noah's ark was odd; but Noah had faith in God.**
5. Close in prayer

SCRIPTURE: Genesis 6:14-16 "So make yourself an ark of cypress wood; make rooms in it and coat it with pitch inside and out. This is how you are to build it: The ark is to be 450 feet long, 75 feet wide and 45 feet high. Make a roof for it and finish the ark to within 18 inches of the top. Put a door in the side of the ark and make lower, middle and upper decks."

MATERIALS: Large box (refrigerator, wardrobe)
Markers or paints
Self-adhesive paper (decorative shelf paper)
Stuffed animals
Bible
Utility knife

Words that are written in **bold** are when you, the parent, are speaking. Feel free to use your own words.

 Big Idea

Using a children's Bible or in your own words, tell the story of Noah and the ark and explain that you are going to build an ark for your family. Parents use the utility knife to cut an opening on the top of the box for the hatch and a door to swing open on one side. Small windows may also be cut.

B Activity

Using the markers and self-adhesive paper, decorate the box to look like a big boat. The boat may be painted instead, but it will need to be done prior to playing this game to allow the paint to dry.

Allow the children to climb in and out of the box as you tell them the story of Noah. Several times during the play time, summarize the story by saying, "Noah had faith in God."

Repeat the activity and this time hide pairs of stuffed animals around the house. With older children, hide the animals in more challenging places.When all the animals have been discovered, fill the ark with children and animals. Parents can make animal sounds outside the ark, drum on the box to represent thunder, and flash the lights to represent lightning.

C Application

While playing these games, ask questions about the story. **How did you feel as we created the ark?** It was fun, etc. **How do you think Noah felt when he was building his ark?** He might have felt confused, and wondered if it was worth all his effort. He probably enjoyed it because he was obeying God. **What might it have been like for Noah and his family in the ark?** It was probably crowded and smelly. They probably hoped the rain would end soon. **What would have happened to Noah and his family if he hadn't obeyed God?** They wouldn't have lived. There wouldn't be any people or animals left today. **What does this story tell us about obeying God?** It is important to obey God. People who obey God will be taken care of.

Lesson 2:
MOSES

 TEACHING GOAL: God protected baby Moses.

1. Play theme song
2. Pray
3. Review last lesson
4. Lesson and discussion
5. Memorize: **Into a basket to avoid detection; placed in a river under God's protection.**
6. Close in prayer

 SCRIPTURE: Exodus 2:3 "But when she could hide him no longer, she got a papyrus basket for him and coated it with tar and pitch. Then she placed the child in it and put it among the reeds along the bank of the Nile."

 MATERIALS: Plastic container
Doll

IN ADVANCE: Secretly fill a bathtub with water, put the doll in the plastic container, and place it in the tub. Don't tell children about this until later.

Words that are written in **bold** are when you, the parent, are speaking. Feel free to use your own words.

 Big Idea

Read the story of Moses from Exodus 2:1-10. Talk about the story and answer questions. **What was the name of the baby?** Moses. **Where did the mommy put Moses?** In a basket in the river. **Why did she do that?** To keep him safe. **Was the mommy sad to have to put her baby in the basket?** Yes. **But was Moses kept safe?** Yes. **Who kept Moses safe?** God. **Who found him?** The Pharaoh's daughter. **And who got to take care of Moses?** His mommy.

Activity

Talk about the story and say, **"Maybe there is a Moses floating in the water in our house. Let's check. Where is there water in our house?"** Check the kitchen, laundry, and then the bathroom(s), finding the baby Moses floating in the bathtub.

Applicaton

God loves us and wants to take care of us. God is always watching and protecting us. Let's spend a few minutes thanking God for protecting us.

Lesson 3:
RUTH

TEACHING GOAL: Family relationships are special.

1. Play theme song
2. Pray
3. Review last lesson
4. Lesson and discussion
5. Memorize: **Christian families stay together; today, tomorrow, and forever.**
6. Close in prayer

SCRIPTURE: Book of Ruth

MATERIALS: Pipe cleaners—7 total: 1 of one color, 3 of another color, and 3 of a third color
Felt—4 colors—green, brown, yellow, and purple work well
1 shoe box
Balloons
Markers
Candy
Scissors or wire cutters

IN ADVANCE: This lesson is called a "Story in a Box." Characters and simple props are stored inside a shoe box. Take items out of the box as you tell the story. The closed box adds suspense and excitement. Repeat the story from time to time. Eventually, children will be able to tell the story themselves using the characters and props.

CHARACTERS: Cut a pipe cleaner in half. With the first half, bend the middle of the pipe cleaner around your finger creating a circular head. Twist the pipe cleaner four times to create the body and the remaining ends form the legs. Take the second half and twist it around the first half several

times, just below the head, to create the arms. Make six characters. One color for Boaz. Use a second color to make Naomi and her two daughters-in-law. A third color to make Naomi's husband and two sons.

PROPS: One color of felt to represent the land of Judah. A second color of felt to represent the land of Moab. A third color, smaller piece to represent a field in Judah. A fourth color of felt cut into small strips to represent corn in the field.

Words that are written in **bold** are when you, the parent, are speaking. Feel free to use your own words.

Big Idea

Tell the story of Ruth and Naomi using the pipe cleaner characters and props. Keep characters and props in the box until they are needed. **Naomi, her husband, and two sons move from Judah to Moab to escape a famine. Have you ever had to move with your family? Why? In Moab, the two sons marry two Moabite women. Then Naomi's husband and two sons die. Naomi leaves to go back home to Judah, and out of loyalty her daughters-in-law, Ruth, goes back with her. Have you ever been loyal and stayed with a friend when you didn't want to or have to stay? Naomi is very sad, but Ruth's friendship and loyalty encourage her. Back in Judah, Ruth starts gleaning the fields of a man named Boaz. Poor people in need of food would go through fields after the harvest and pick up what the harvesters did not get—that's called gleaning. Boaz and the people of Judah watched how Ruth looked after Naomi. Did you know people watch how you behave with your brother, sister, mom, and dad? What do you think other people see? Because of Ruth's kindness and loyalty, Boaz marries Ruth. Ruth is the great-grandmother of King David. Do you know your great-grandmother?**

Ruth encouraged Naomi. When Naomi was upset, Ruth stayed with her. As family members, we need to encourage and comfort each other.

 Activity

In Ruth 1:14 the Bible says Ruth clung to Naomi. There is a special relationship between family members. Other people will come and go, but we are family members for life, forever.

It is important to be loyal and honor the special loving relationship we have as family members. Even when we disagree or get upset, we need to forgive and love each other.

CLINGING RUTH

OPTION 1: Each child gets an inflated balloon with a stick figure of Ruth drawn on it. Rub the balloon on your hair and have a race across the room with the balloon clinging to your clothes. If the balloon falls off, then you have to go back to the start, rub the balloon on your hair, and try to cross the room again.

OPTION 2: If necessary, use a small piece of tape to hold the balloon on.

OPTION 3: With larger groups, teams of two family members can run holding the balloon between their hips.

 **Application**

Naomi and Ruth were poor when they moved back to Judah. Those people with fields of food would leave some food in the field for the poor. It is important to share what we have with the poor. Divide the yard into one section for each child. You may use a rope to divide the sections. Hide several pieces of candy in the grass. **We are going to pretend these were fields of candy. The harvesters have come through and taken most of the candy, but maybe they left a few pieces in the fields.**

The story of Ruth and Naomi teaches us that family members stick together. In good times and hard times, families stick together. We share because families stick together. We take turns doing what others don't like to do because families stick together. Think of five things we did together last week because, "Families stick together."

Lesson 4:
PRISCILLA AND AQUILA—
THE GIFT OF HOSPITALITY

TEACHING GOAL: Showing hospitality is a privilege.

1. Play theme song
2. Pray
3. Review last lesson
4. Lesson and discussion
5. Memorize: **Hospitality is a gift; it gives others a lift.**
6. Close in prayer

SCRIPTURE: Acts 18:1-2 "After this, Paul left Athens and went to Corinth. There he met a Jew named Aquila, a native of Pontus, who had recently come from Italy with his wife Priscilla, because Claudius had ordered all the Jews to leave Rome."

1 Corinthians 16:19 "Aquila and Priscilla greet you warmly in the Lord, and so does the church that meets at their house."

1 Peter 4:9 "Offer hospitality to one another without grumbling."

MATERIALS: Bed sheets
Cord or thin rope
Clothespins
Tea or other drink
Tea set or cups, saucers, and plates
Cookies or crackers

Words that are written in **bold** are when you, the parent, are speaking. Feel free to use your own words.

A Big Idea

Using the sheets and working with the children, build a tent large enough for the whole family. **TENT OPTIONS:** 1. Outside you can attach the sheets to a clothesline, fence, or poles. 2. Inside you can drape the sheets over chairs, tables, and other furniture. **SAFETY FIRST:** Avoid using too much tension that may pull down furniture.

While setting up the tent, tell a story from the Bible about three tent-makers: **Paul, one of the early Christians who lived almost 2,000 years ago, traveled to a city called Corinth where he met two other Christians named Priscilla and Aquila. Paul, Priscilla, and Aquila were all tent-makers. Lots of people lived in tents back in the days of Jesus, so being a tent-maker was a lot like being a home builder today. Priscilla and Aquila invited Paul to live with them. Paul would preach at church on the weekend and make tents with Priscilla and Aquila during the week.**

When Paul had to leave Corinth and go to a new city called Ephesus, Priscilla and Aquila went with him. Priscilla and Aquila provided a place for Paul to stay when he was in Ephesus. Priscilla and Aquila also started a church that met in their home.

They had what is called the gift of hospitality. Do you know what hospitality means? Listen to their answers. **When you invite someone over for dinner—that's hospitality. When someone is sick and you fix them a meal—that's hospitality. When you see someone who looks lonely and you talk to them—that's hospitality. Hospitality is sharing with others who are in need.**

God wants us to practice the gift of hospitality—sharing with others who are in need. In the Bible (1 Peter 4:9) **it says, "Offer hospitality to one another without grumbling."**

 **Activity**

After the tent is set up say: **We're going to practice the gift of hospitality. Just like Paul, Priscilla, and Aquila we have built a tent. Now each person will have a turn being (Priscilla for the girls and Aquila for the boys). Whoever is Priscilla or Aquila will serve everyone tea and a cookie.** Take turns having the children pour tea and add sugar and/or milk. Give out a cookie or a cracker. Explain that they are practicing hospitality by serving others before themselves and meeting others' needs of thirst and hunger.

 Application

God gives each of us spiritual gifts. Parents and others who know their spiritual gifts can share what they are and how they use them. For example:

MOM—HOSPITALITY She makes meals for friends who are sick.

DAD—GIVING He teaches us to give money to the homeless and hurting.

GRAMMY—JOY She makes people feel good and happy when she is around.

GRANDPA—TEACHING He leads a Sunday School class.

Talk about other spiritual gifts listed in the Bible:

TEACHING: Who do we know that teaches at church?

PREACHING: Who do we know that is a preacher?

SERVICE: Who do we know that helps others?

MISSIONARY: Who do we know that is a missionary?

Lesson 5:
SOAK IT UP!

TEACHING GOAL: When we fill our lives with the teachings of Jesus, then we will bear the fruit of the Spirit.

1. Play theme song
2. Pray
3. Review last lesson
4. Lesson and discussion
5. Memorize: **Soak up Jesus through and through; that's what I am going to do!**
6. Close in prayer

SCRIPTURE: Psalm 1:2-3 "But his delight is in the law of the LORD, and on his law he meditates day and night. He is like a tree planted by streams of water, which yields its fruit in season and whose leaf does not wither. Whatever he does prospers."

Galatians 5:22-23 "But the fruit of the Spirit is love, joy, peace, patience, kindness, goodness, faithfulness, gentleness and self-control."

MATERIALS: Celery stalks (light green) with leaves
Red or blue food coloring
Glass and water

IN ADVANCE: Do the following activity together as a family 45 minutes before starting Family Time. Fill a glass with a couple inches of water and add food coloring to the water. The more color in the water, the better. Cut the bottom off of a large rib of celery. Do not cut off the celery leaves. Set the bottom of the celery in the glass of colored water and then set it out of sight in a warm place.

Words that are written in **bold** are when you, the parent, are speaking. Feel free to use your own words.

 Big Idea

When traveling across a prairie, there are unobstructed views where you can see for miles and miles. Sometimes, looking across the prairie, lines of trees can be seen, usually located in valleys or between hills. Why are there only a few trees, and why do they grow together in lines that weave through valleys across the prairie? Listen to answers. The trees grow along rivers and lakes where they can get the water they need to live.

The Bible describes people who follow God by using the phrase, "like trees planted along the riverbank." Listen to Psalm 1:2-3. Read Psalm 1:2-3. We are the trees, God is the river, and what is the water that we soak up? Listen to answers. The water is God's direction for our lives—the Bible. When we do what the Bible says, like following his commands, we are following God's law and doing what God wants us to do. We are like a tree planted next to the river that bears fruit, whose leaves never wither and who will prosper. What kind of fruit will we bear? Listen to their answers. Listen to Galatians 5:22-23. Ask someone to read Galatians 5:22-23. What fruit does Galatians tell us we will bear? Love, joy, peace patience, kindness, goodness, faithfulness, gentleness, and self-control. Give examples of fruit you see in your life. Can you give examples of fruit you wish you had more of in your life?

B Activity

Bring out the celery. The rib and leaves will have soaked up some of the color. You can see that the celery looks different. In the same way, when we do what the Bible teaches—model our thoughts, words, and actions after Jesus' example—our lives will look different.

Consider leaving the celery rib in the food color overnight. More of the color will soak up into the leaves. Looking at the celery rib the next day will reinforce the lesson.

 Application

When the celery turns a color it's because the water is flowing inside of it. Normally we can't see the juices flowing inside. The food coloring makes it easier to see what's happening.

The same thing happens in each of our lives. When we read the Bible it helps us on the inside. In fact, the Bible uses that picture of a tree near a river to describe the person who is receiving nourishment from the Bible.

Keep in mind that every time you read, listen to, or memorize the scriptures, something very important happens inside of you.

Lesson 6:
SPIRITUAL GROWTH

 TEACHING GOAL: We need to keep growing spiritually throughout our lives.

1. Play theme song
2. Pray
3. Review last lesson
4. Lesson and discussion
5. Memorize: **Spiritually we grow; when God we know.**
6. Close in prayer

 SCRIPTURE: Philippians 1:6 "He who began a good work in you will carry it on to completion until the day of Christ Jesus."

1 Peter 2:2 "Like newborn babies, crave pure spiritual milk, so that by it you may grow up in your salvation."

 MATERIALS: Wood molding: 6' to 7', one piece per child
White paint
Marker

Words that are written in **bold** are when you, the parent, are speaking. Feel free to use your own words.

A▶ Big Idea

Mark the piece of molding with your child's height at each birthday, showing physical growth. You may have to find these heights in medical records or a baby book if you have not been keeping a growth chart. Mark the height of your child on the day you do this Family Time. If you don't know the actual height of your child at various ages, you can guess or imagine. Kids will get the point.

Activity

In the same way we track physical growth, we can keep track of our spiritual growth. Invite children to help you paint the pieces of molding with white paint. Flip the piece of molding over and divide into 20 equal sections representing 20 years. Keep track of events that mark spiritual growth.

Birth	Learning to pray
First mission project	Salvation
Dedication	Learning to give
First testimony	Baptism
First communion	Memorizing a Bible verse
Names of Sunday School teachers	

If a child stops growing physically, parents seek medical help. If a child stops growing spiritually, then parents need to seek spiritual help.

Application

Hang the moldings where the children will see them from time to time. On birthdays mark physical growth. On the other side of the molding, as your children grow in their faith, mark events that symbolize their spiritual growth. Feel free to add new milestones that demonstrate spiritual growth.

Talk about the scripture for this lesson and describe ways that we can grow spiritually.

Lesson 7:
MESSAGES TO GOD

TEACHING GOAL: God lives in heaven.

1. Play theme song
2. Pray
3. Review last lesson
4. Lesson and discussion
5. Memorize: **We send our love; to God in heaven above.**
6. Close in prayer

SCRIPTURE: Deuteronomy 26:15 "Look down from heaven, your holy dwelling place, and bless your people."

MATERIALS: One inflated helium balloon per family member
Markers

Words that are written in **bold** are when you, the parent, are speaking. Feel free to use your own words.

Big Idea

Read the scripture above. **From heaven God watches over us when we are sleeping, playing, eating—all the time. He knows when we do what is right and when we do what is wrong. God loves us very much.**

 Activity

Let's tell God how much we love him. Draw a picture, write "I love you," or trace your handprint on a helium balloon. One at a time, release the balloons outside and watch until it disappears into heaven.

Take pictures of the balloons and of your family letting them go.

Application

Is heaven a real place? Yes, the Bible tells us so. **God lives in heaven but is he so far away that he can't see us?** No. He can see us and he even says that he is close to us.

God blesses us in a lot of ways. He give us all kinds of gifts. Can you think of some of the ways God blesses us? Food, flowers, sunshine, friends, etc.

God wants us to bless him too. We do that by telling him often that we love him. We also take time to thank him for his gifts to us.

Let's take time now and thank God for his gifts to us.

Lesson 8:
A ROOM IN HEAVEN

 TEACHING GOAL: Jesus went to heaven to prepare a place for us.

1. Play theme song
2. Pray
3. Review last lesson
4. Lesson and discussion
5. Memorize: **Jesus left the tomb; and went to heaven to prepare my room.**
6. Close in prayer

 SCRIPTURE: John 14:2-4 "In my Father's house are many rooms; if it were not so, I would have told you. I am going there to prepare a place for you. And if I go and prepare a place for you, I will come back and take you to be with me that you also may be where I am. You know the way to the place where I am going."

 MATERIALS: Clothes line, strong string, or thin rope
Bed sheets and clothespins

IN ADVANCE: This will take some time but it is worth it! Pick a space (basement, guest room, kid's room) where the created "mansion" can stay up for a couple days. Kids will enjoy hours of playing in the "mansion" after Family Time.

Turn a room in the house into a maze leading to several spaces called "rooms." To begin run the string, cord, or rope back and forth across the room about chest high. Attach the rope to closet rods, bed posts, doors, etc. (Safety First! Do not attach it to anything that can be pulled down onto kids playing below.)

Create a web with lines running in all directions across the room. Next, take as many sheets as you can find and use clothespins to fasten them to the lines in such a way that you create passages that lead to several spaces called "rooms." Create enough rooms so that you'll have one for each child. If you have extra sheets you can lay them across the top of the rope-web creating a sheet-ceiling. Be creative. Boxes can be used as tunnels. You are creating an elaborate fort made from sheets.

If possible, keep the "mansion" a secret.

Words that are written in **bold** are when you, the parent, are speaking. Feel free to use your own words.

 Big Idea

Start the Family Time in a room away from the "mansion." Ask each child to bring a favorite toy or personal item. Read John 14:2-4. **When Jesus went up in the clouds after being raised from the dead, He went to heaven to prepare a place for everyone who believes in him.**

 Activity

In the same way that Jesus is preparing a place for us, I have been working to prepare a special place for you. This place is a mansion made of sheets. There are passageways and secret rooms. I've picked a special room for each one of you. You will know which room is yours because it will have one of your toys in it. Just like Jesus went to heaven and promised to come back and get us, I need you to give me one of your toys so I can go to prepare your room. Stay here and I will come back and get you.

Come back and invite the kids one at a time to go into the mansion and find his or her special room. You may choose to ask them if they can recite the memorization before they can go back and play in the maze. The kids will love playing in the maze for as long as you will leave it up!

 **Application**

Take time to remind children that Jesus is preparing a special place for those who believe in him. That's important because it demonstrates that God loves us and cares for us.

Lesson 9:
WIDE AND NARROW ROADS

 TEACHING GOAL: Being a follower of Christ is not always easy or popular.

1. Play theme song
2. Pray
3. Review last lesson
4. Lesson and discussion
5. Memorize: **Choose today; the narrow way.**
6. Close in prayer

 SCRIPTURE: Matthew 7:13-14 "Enter through the narrow gate. For wide is the gate and broad is the road that leads to destruction, and many enter through it. But small is the gate and narrow the road that leads to life, and only a few find it."

Luke 10:30-35 A man traveling to Jericho was attacked and left for dead. A priest and Levite passed that man without helping but a Samaritan stopped and helped the injured man.

 MATERIALS: Section of sidewalk
Narrow board on top of bricks or line in the dirt
Reward: piece of candy, hug, etc.

Words that are written in **bold** are when you, the parent, are speaking. Feel free to use your own words.

 Big Idea

Being a Christian is not always popular. Sometimes in order to do what pleases God Christians have to do things that are not easy.

I am going to tell each of you a story that involves making a choice. After you hear the story I want you to tell me which choice would be easiest and which choice would Christ want us to make.

1. You go to the park where a group of boys are picking teams for a game of soccer. Soccer is your favorite game. There is room for only one more player but there are two kids left, you and a new boy who just moved to the neighborhood. Since the other players already know you, you could yell "pick me" and you are pretty sure that they would pick you over the new boy. What should you do? What is the easy choice? What is the Christ-like choice?

2. 100 dollars drops out of the pocket of a stranger walking down the street. The man doesn't know he dropped the money. What should you do? What is the easy choice? What is the Christ-like choice?

3. Kids at school are making fun of another student for being a Christian. The kids don't know that you are a Christian too. What should you do? What is the easy choice? What is the Christ-like choice?

4. God tells us in the Bible that we are to give generously to others in need. Your family has just enough money for food. What should you do? What is the easy choice? What is the Christ-like choice?

5. There is a boy your age in the neighborhood who is poor, dirty, smelly, and doesn't seem to have any friends. What should you do? What is the easy choice? What is the Christ-like choice?

6. Make up more stories if needed. Give each person a turn to answer the questions. Allow time for discussion and allow kids to suggest other solutions to the problems.

B Activity

Choose a section of sidewalk to use as a path. Mark off a section at least ten feet long with a "start" and a "finish." Next to the sidewalk create a narrow walkway. You may want to use boards balanced above the ground on bricks, a string stretched out across the ground, or even a line drawn in the dirt.

Read Matthew 7:13-14. **The sidewalk represents the "wide road." The boards represent the "narrow road." Two children at a time are going to race each other. One will race down the sidewalk while the other runs down the boards** (or along the line in the dirt). **The one racing down the boards must stay on the boards at all times, while the one racing down the sidewalk needs to stay on the sidewalk.** Give each child a chance to race one or more times. The child on the narrow path should lose, while the child running on the less restricted sidewalk should win. Stand at the end of the narrow path and give the child who completes the race a reward (candy or hug) even though they were not the fastest.

Was it easier or harder to run on the wide path? Why? Listen to their answers. **Did you notice that I gave a reward (candy or hug) to the one who finished walking along the narrow path? Why do you think I did that?** Listen to their answers.

 **Application**

This is a paraphrase of Matthew 7:13-14 that you might find helpful: Wide is the road that leads to trouble, narrow is the road that leads to doing what is right. **It may be easier to do what everyone else is doing, the wide road, but it leads to trouble. It may be harder to do what Christ wants us to do, the narrow road, but there is a reward at the end. I gave you a hug/candy as the reward in this game. What is the reward at the end of life for Christians?** Heaven. **It's worth taking the harder road in life, living like Jesus, because there is the reward of heaven at the end. When we face decisions every day we need to ask, "What would Jesus do?"**

Lesson 10:
LOST SHEEP HIDE-AND-SEEK

TEACHING GOAL: Jesus cares about us when we are lost.

1. Play theme song
2. Pray
3. Review last lesson
4. Lesson and discussion
5. Memorize: **Jesus is our shepherd; when we are lost he comes to find us.**
6. Close in prayer

SCRIPTURE: Luke 15:4-7 "Suppose one of you has a hundred sheep and loses one of them. Does he not leave the ninety-nine in the open country and go after the lost sheep until he finds it? And when he finds it, he joyfully puts it on his shoulders and goes home. Then he calls his friends and neighbors together and says, 'Rejoice with me; I have found my lost sheep.' I tell you that in the same way there will be more rejoicing in heaven over one sinner who repents."

MATERIALS: No materials needed

Words that are written in **bold** are when you, the parent, are speaking. Feel free to use your own words.

Big Idea

Jesus liked to tell stories. One of his famous stories was about a shepherd who was watching over 100 sheep. After counting the sheep, the shepherd found that one was missing. The shepherd left the 99 sheep and went looking for the lost one. When he found the missing sheep, he carried it home on his shoulders. The shepherd had a party with his friends to celebrate finding the lost sheep.

What do you think it would feel like to be the one lost sheep? Listen to their answers. Scary, lonely. **How do you think the shepherd felt when he found out that one of his sheep was missing?** Worried. **How do you think the 99 sheep felt when the shepherd left to find the lost sheep?** Okay because there were so many of them. Nervous. Happy for the lost sheep.

In the story of the lost sheep, Jesus is the shepherd. The 99 sheep represent people who already know and believe in Jesus. The one lost sheep is someone who doesn't yet believe in Jesus. Here's what the story means: Jesus is our shepherd and when we are lost he cares and comes to find us. Can you repeat that? Lead them in saying, **Jesus is our shepherd...and when we are lost...he cares and comes to find us.**

B ► Activity

We are going to play "Lost Sheep Hide-and-Seek." Select one person to be the shepherd and another person to be the lost sheep. Each person can have a turn being the shepherd and the lost sheep. The shepherd will close his eyes and count to 25. The lost sheep has 25 seconds to hide and then the shepherd will come to find him. Every time a shepherd brings back a lost sheep repeat the meaning of Jesus' story: Jesus is our shepherd and when we are lost he cares and comes to find us.

 **Application**

Friends and family who don't believe in Jesus are lost and we can ask Jesus to go find them. When someone we know becomes a Christian, we can have a party and celebrate!

Even when we are Christians we sometimes lose our way. When we make bad choices and sin, it's like being lost. We need Jesus to help us make good decisions and follow him.

Lesson 11:
DANCING DAVID AND MERRY MIRIAM

TEACHING GOAL: There is joy in the Lord.

1. Play theme song
2. Pray
3. Review last lesson
4. Lesson and discussion
5. Memorize: **Praise his name, it's only right; to dance with joy, with all your might!**
6. Close in prayer

SCRIPTURE: Psalm 149:3-4 "Let them praise his name with dancing and make music to him with tambourine and harp. For the LORD takes delight in his people."

Psalm 150:4 "Praise him with tambourine and dancing."

Ecclesiastes 3:4 "A time to mourn and a time to dance."

Lamentations 5:15 "Joy is gone from our hearts; our dancing has turned to mourning."

2 Samuel 6:14-15 (The ark of the covenant returns to Jerusalem) "David, wearing a linen ephod, danced before the LORD with all his might, while he and the entire house of Israel brought up the ark of the LORD with shouts and the sound of trumpets."

Exodus 15:20 (The Red Sea closes on Pharaoh's army) "Then Miriam the prophetess, Aaron's sister, took a tambourine in her hand, and all the women followed her, with tambourines and dancing."

Psalm 30:11 "You turned my wailing into dancing."

MATERIALS: 1 piece of paper
Pen or pencil
Sissors
Aluminum pie pans, disposable, each child needs 2
Plexiglass (obtained from local hardware store)
Wide tape of any type
4 pennies per child
1 facial tissue

IN ADVANCE: On the paper, draw simple figures of David and Miriam about ³/₄″ tall x ¹/₂″ wide.

Words that are written in **bold** are when you, the parent, are speaking. Feel free to use your own words.

 Big Idea

When someone dies, that person's friends and family are very, very sad. This very deep sadness is called mourning. Do you know what the opposite of mourning is? Happy. **The Bible says that the opposite of mourning is joy and dancing. Let me read you some of the Bible verses that talks about mourning, joy, and dancing.** Read the scriptures listed at the beginning of this lesson.

Have you ever been so excited about something that you actually danced? Riding an amusement park ride. Scoring a goal or touchdown. **In the Bible, people got so excited about praising God and about the things that God had done for them that they would dance. David was so excited about the ark of the covenant returning to Jerusalem that he danced before the Lord with all of his might!**

After God made a way for the Israelites to be freed from slavery under Pharaoh, he parted the Red Sea so that the Israelites could escape. The Israelites were thrilled and amazed at how God had saved them. Miriam, Moses' sister, grabbed her tambourine and began to dance.

Activity

Allow children to cut out the paper characters you prepared, if capable. Place the paper characters into an aluminum pie pan. Cover the top of the pie pan with the Plexiglas. Vigorously rub the tissue on the top of the Plexiglas to create static electricity. "David" and "Miriam" will dance. If the characters seem to get stuck, lift the Plexiglas and remove them and begin again. Discuss how our joy in the Lord is pleasing to him.

Place four pennies in a pie pan. Cover with another pie pan and tape securely around all of the edges to hold pans together to form a tambourine. Pretend you are Miriam and the Israelites, dancing joyfully as you march around your home.

 **Application**

We can worship God in a variety of ways. Sometimes we sing, clap, stand up, or raise our hands. Miriam and David are examples of people in the Bible who were so excited about worship that they danced before the Lord. Whatever way we worship it needs to come from our hearts. God is the one we are worshiping. He wants us to enjoy the worship and lift up our hearts to him.

Lesson 12:
MESSENGER ANGELS

 TEACHING GOAL: God uses angels to deliver his messages.

1. Play theme song
2. Pray
3. Review last lesson
4. Lesson and discussion
5. Memorize: **Angels from above; deliver God's messages of love.**
6. Close in prayer

 SCRIPTURE: Luke 2:10 (Angels announce the birth of Jesus to the shepherds) "But the angel said to them, 'Do not be afraid. I bring you good news.'"

Luke 1:13 "But the angel said to him: 'Do not be afraid, Zechariah; your prayer has been heard.'"

Hebrews 13:2 "Do not forget to entertain strangers, for by so doing some people have entertained angels without knowing it."

Genesis 16:10 Angel delivers message of blessing.

Genesis 22:11-12 Angel delivers message of protection.

Exodus 23:20 Angel as guide providing direction.

Judges 6 Angel brings a message of God's presence.

Acts 10:4-6 Angel arranges meeting.

 MATERIALS: Paper, pen, tape, and yellow marker/crayon

Words that are written in **bold** are when you, the parent, are speaking. Feel free to use your own words.

Big Idea

God uses angels to deliver his
messages to people. Several times
angels were used to announce the
birth of babies: Isaac, John the
Baptist, Jesus. Angels were also
used to bring messages about war,
to provide directions, and to
announce a blessing from God.

There is one message that
angels delivered over and over again, "Do not be afraid."

Have you ever seen or received a message from an angel?
Listen to their answers. **Here is a very interesting
comment about angels that comes from the book of
Hebrews in the Bible. It says to be kind to strangers
because in doing so, some people have been kind to angels
without even knowing it. It is possible that God has sent
his angels to help us without us even knowing it!**

 Activity

**Using the design for a paper airplane we are going to
make a messenger angel.** Following the directions provided,
make a stub-nose, dart-style paper airplane.

Using the yellow marker, draw an angel on the airplane's
wings: Make an oval halo at the stub-nose tip, a circle head,
wings that follow the wings of the plane, and a rectangle
shaped lower body.

Write a message on the body of the plane under the angel
drawing or unfold the plane to write longer messages before
refolding. The messages can be things that angels said in the
Bible:

Do not be afraid.
God hears your prayers.

Or, you may want to write an encouraging verse or another message that models something God might want to say to us. Fly the "angels" back and forth in a game of catch or aiming at a target.

◀ Application

Tell the children that after they go to bed, you are going to fly an angel into their room with a special message for the next day. When they wake up they need to try and find the angel and read their message. Message ideas:

- "Whether you eat or drink or whatever you do, do it all for the glory of God." **1 Corinthians 10:31**

- Be encouraged! **1 Thessalonians 4:18**

- God loves you! **John 3:16**

Have the child bring you the airplane in the morning so that you can read the message.

MAKING AN "ANGEL" AIRPLANE
STEP 1:
Take an 8¹/2″ x 11″ sheet of paper and fold it in half, lengthwise.

STEP 2:
Fold down the top two corners, toward the inside of the plane—making the edge of the paper meet the fold.

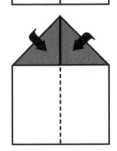

STEP 3:
Fold down the sides again, making the edges of the fold meet each other in the center.

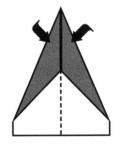

STEP 4:

Fold 1″ of the tip down inside the plane, making a blunt nose.

STEP 5:

Fold the sides together so that the two outside edges meet at the top and the folded tip is inside.

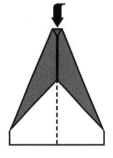

STEP 6:

Fold the top edge of each side down to match the bottom fold, that creates the wings. You now have a stub-nose, dart-style paper airplane.

STEP 7:

Use a small piece of tape to hold the back of the plane together.

Lesson 13:
LITTLE THINGS BECOME GOD THINGS

TEACHING GOAL: God wants to include us in his adventure.

1. Play theme song
2. Pray
3. Review last lesson
4. Lesson and discussion
5. Memorize: **Trust God's way; enjoy an adventure today.**
6. Close in prayer

SCRIPTURE: Matthew 17:24-27 "After Jesus and his disciples arrived in Capernaum, the collectors of the two-drachma tax came to Peter and asked, 'Doesn't your teacher pay the temple tax?' 'Yes, he does,' he replied. When Peter came into the house, Jesus was the first to speak. 'What do you think, Simon?' he asked. 'From whom do the kings of the earth collect duty and taxes—from their own sons or from others?' 'From others,' Peter answered. 'Then the sons are exempt,' Jesus said to him. 'But so that we may not offend them, go to the lake and throw out your line. Take the first fish you catch; open its mouth and you will find a four-drachma coin. Take it and give it to them for my tax and yours.'"

MATERIALS: Foil-wrapped candy "coins" or a variety of coins

IN ADVANCE: Hide candy or coins around the house (vary the difficulty of the hiding places based on the ages of your kids).

Words that are written in **bold** are when you, the parent, are speaking. Feel free to use your own words.

A Big Idea

Sometimes God asks us to do things in order to prove himself to us or to help our faith grow. When he wants to do something special in our lives, he wants us to trust him. It would be very easy for God to just give us what we want or need whenever we asked him, but that wouldn't help us learn to trust him. We show our trust and faith by doing what he asks, even if we are scared to do it or think God won't give us the answer we want.

B Activity

Tell the story from Matthew 17:24-27 in your own words, stressing that Jesus and Peter had no money to pay the tax that was due. **Jesus asked Peter to go out and fish, then bring back the coin that he would find in the fish's mouth. Peter was a fisherman; he knew how to fish. Was Jesus asking Peter to do something that was hard for him?** No. **Do you think Peter had ever found a coin in the mouth of a fish before?** Probably not. **How do you think Peter felt being asked to go fish and look for a coin in the mouth of the first fish he caught?** He may have thought Jesus was crazy for asking him to do this because it wasn't normal to find money in the mouth of a fish. **The coin Peter found was exactly enough money to pay for the taxes for both of them.**

God used Peter's small action of fishing to perform this big miracle. There were three miraculous parts: 1) finding money in a fish at all, 2) finding the money in the first fish he caught, and 3) that the money was the exact amount needed. God worked out all of the details and all Peter had to do was obey and go fishing. What a miracle of God!

Could Jesus have just spoken and the money would have appeared in his hand? Yes. **Why do you think Jesus wanted Peter to fish instead?** To let Peter be a part of the adventure. Following Jesus' instructions helped Peter's faith grow. **Could Peter have said, "No! We need money now, and this is no time to go fishing!"** Yes. **If he had said that, what do you think the outcome would have been?** Peter would have missed out on an important lesson and being part of the exciting miracle. Jesus would have been disappointed that Peter missed out, too. **What do you think Peter thought and felt the next time Jesus asked him to do something that may have sounded crazy?** He probably felt excited to see what God would do. He had faith that it would turn out just like Jesus said it would.

I have hidden coins around the house. I want you to go find them. You can keep whatever you find in the next two/five/ten minutes. (You can vary the time depending upon how quickly the coins are found. You may also hide coins in separate rooms if the ages of your children would make a combined hunt poorly matched.) After the coins are found, continue the discussion.

Was it hard to run around the house finding the coins? No. **Did I ask you to do something you didn't know how to do or that was too hard for you?** No. **You're right. It was easy to find the coins, but I didn't just give them to you. I am your father (mother/grandparent) and I knew just how to hide the coins so that it wouldn't be too hard for you.**
I didn't just give the coins to you because I knew it would be more fun and interesting to make a game out of it.

God can just give us things, but he wants us to be a part of the adventure with him! When God gives us something to do, he knows just how much to give us so that it won't be too hard for us.

◖▸ Application

When I asked you to find the coins that I had hidden around the house, was it hard? No. Was it more fun to hunt for them than if I'd just placed the coins in your hand? Yes.

God wants us to be a part of his adventures, too. Sometimes we think if he asks us to do something it will be too hard. Often God asks us to be faithful doing what we already know how to do, so that he can perform a miracle. As we obey God in the little things, our faith will grow just like Peter's. It will be an exciting adventure to see what God will do. Don't be afraid to do something when God asks you to—he is your heavenly father and he knows just exactly how much you can do!

Lesson 14:
LIGHT IN THE DARKNESS

TEACHING GOAL: Christians are called to be light in a dark world.

1. Play theme song
2. Pray
3. Review last lesson
4. Lesson and discussion
5. Memorize: **Jesus the light; in our life shines bright.**
6. Close in prayer

SCRIPTURE: Matthew 5:14-16 "You are the light of the world. A city on a hill cannot be hidden. Neither do people light a lamp and put it under a bowl. Instead they put it on its stand, and it gives light to everyone in the house. In the same way, let your light shine before men, that they may see your good deeds and praise your Father in heaven."

John 1:4-5 "In him was life, and that life was the light of men. The light shines in the darkness, but the darkness has not understood it."

Acts 26:17-18 (The conversion of Paul) "I am sending you to them to open their eyes and turn them from darkness to light, and from the power of Satan to God."

Galatians 5:22-23 "But the fruit of the Spirit is love, joy, peace, patience, kindness, goodness, faithfulness, gentleness and self-control."

MATERIALS: Glow-in-the-dark items large enough to write on (stars, bugs, shapes)
Marker

Words that are written in **bold** are when you, the parent, are speaking. Feel free to use your own words.

A ▶ Big Idea

What are some things that shine? Sun, moon, stars, shiny jewelry, flashlight.

Jesus tells us that as Christians in this world we are a light shining in the darkness. How do Christians "shine" in a world that is dark? Give them a chance to answer.

I am going to read some short sentences from the Bible. See if you can find the answers to these questions. (Read the scriptures provided above.)

Who is to be the light in the world? Followers of Jesus. **Who is the source of the light?** Jesus. **What does it mean that the world is dark?** People who do not follow Jesus. **What kind of things in our lives make us shine to others?** Love, joy, peace, patience, kindness, goodness, faithfulness, gentleness, and self-control.

B ▶ Activity

Using the marker write the words love, joy, peace, patience, kindness, goodness, faithfulness, gentleness, and self-control on the glow-in-the-dark items. Talk about these characteristics as you write them.

Hold the glow items up to a light. Then hide them in a dark room and let the kids take turns finding them. Hide them so at least a part will glow and be seen. The older the children, the harder you can make it to find the glowing items.

- The light represents Jesus.
- We are the items that glow.
- The glow from the items represents characteristics of Jesus shining in our lives.
- The dark room represents the world that does not know Jesus.

Our lives are to shine, drawing others to the love of Jesus. People should see something different in our life that attracts them to know more about our faith.

OPTIONAL: Consider keeping the glow items in the dark prior to the activity. During the first turn, hide the items that have been stored in the dark. There will be very little glow and it will be much harder to find them. Then hold them in the light and show how much easier it is to find them when they have been exposed to the light.

 Application

As Christians we need to stay close to Jesus, the light. How can we stay close to Jesus? Reading or hearing the Bible. Prayer. Church. Family Time. When we stay close to Jesus and do what he says, then our lives will shine more. When Christians do not stay close to Jesus but expose themselves only to the world, then they lose their shine. It is hard to tell these Christians from the world around them.

Lesson 15:
A STRONG TOWER

 TEACHING GOAL: There is power in the name of Jesus.

1. Play theme song
2. Pray
3. Review last lesson
4. Lesson and discussion
5. Memorize: **Jesus' name, a tower with power.**
6. Close in prayer

 SCRIPTURE: Proverbs 18:10 "The name of the LORD is a strong tower; the righteous run to it and are safe."

 MATERIALS: No materials needed.

Words that are written in **bold** are when you, the parent, are speaking. Feel free to use your own words.

Big Idea

Read Proverbs 18:10. **How can a name keep you safe?** Parents sign their names to take their kids out of school or Sunday School class. ID's are used to check names before getting on an airplane. We write our name on clothes to keep them from being lost. **Did you ever think that the name "Jesus" has the power to keep you safe?** When scared, we can pray to Jesus for safety. The Bible teaches us that if we feel like something bad is happening, we can call on the name of Jesus to protect us. **It is important to remember that there is power in the name of Jesus.**

 Activity

We're going to play a special game of tag. This game will help us to remember that the name of Jesus has power to keep us safe. The verse we read says, "The name of

the Lord is a strong tower." Let's pick something tall to be our tower and that will be "base." Pick a tree, part of a swing set, light pole, etc. to be base. **If you are being chased, you can go to the tower that is base and yell "Jesus." By yelling "Jesus" and touching the tower, the tagger cannot get you. If the tagger touches you when you're not touching the tower, then you become the tagger.** Play the game of tag and when you are finished, remind everyone of the memorized theme: Jesus' name, a tower with power.

Application

What is a time when you might feel afraid or in need and want to call on the name of Jesus? When you're afraid, think you're lost, afraid of the dark, or when you've lost your shoes or toy.

Talk about the importance of calling on the name of the Lord for needs. You might even tell your children stories of answered prayers to encourage them to pray as well.

Lesson 16:
HONOR VOLLEYBALL

 TEACHING GOAL: We can show honor to others with our words.

1. Play theme song
2. Pray
3. Review last lesson
4. Lesson and discussion
5. Memorize: **Use words that reflect; honor and respect.**
6. Close in prayer

 SCRIPTURE: 1 Peter 2:17 "Show proper respect to everyone."

Romans 12:10 "Honor one another above yourselves."

 MATERIALS: Balloon
Marker
String, two chairs
Open area

Words that are written in **bold** are when you, the parent, are speaking. Feel free to use your own words.

 Big Idea

The Bible tells us to show proper respect to everyone and to honor one another above ourselves. We want to create an atmosphere of honor and respect within our family. There are many ways to show respect and to honor someone: a smile, a pleasant tone of voice, and the words we use.

Sometimes I say, "Don't use that tone of voice." Or, "Ask nicely." Today we're going to play a special game of volleyball that will help us learn words that show honor and respect to each other.

First we need to make a list of these words because we're going to need them to play the game. Let me give you a couple examples of what I'm talking about and then everyone can add to the list. Thank You. Please. Yes Mom. Praise kids who suggest longer phrases that are compliments and positive; however, what you need for this game is a list of respectful words and phrases that are one to three words long. More examples:

Nice meal	Honey	Excuse me	May I
I'm sorry	Great job	You're welcome	Forgive me
Yes Dad	Good point	No thank you	Pardon me
Of course	Right away		

 Activity

Blow up the balloon. Write the words from your list on the balloon. Create a "net" in the open area by tying a string between two chairs.

Hit the balloon volley-ball back and forth over the net. Each time you hit the volleyball, you need to say one of the words from your list that is written on the balloon. If someone comes up with a new phrase like "nice shot," then use the marker and add it to the balloon.

 Application

Throughout the coming week, model the polite and respectful words. Encourage your kids to use the words as well. Talk about honor and how we treat each other with value. As we do, it adds a pleasant atmosphere to our home.

Lesson 17:
LET JESUS HELP

TEACHING GOAL: We can accomplish more with God than we can alone.

1. Play theme song
2. Pray
3. Review last lesson
4. Lesson and discussion
5. Memorize: **Without Jesus we'll just blow and blow. Try with Jesus; he'll make things grow.**
6. Close in prayer

SCRIPTURE: Luke 5:4-11 Story of Jesus telling Peter to fish. Peter had already tried without success but does it again for Jesus, this time successfully.

John 21:3-8 Story of the disciples fishing without success again and Jesus tells them to cast their nets on the other side of the boat, this time with success.

Philippians 4:13 "I can do everything through him who gives me strength."

MATERIALS: 2 balloons—1 with a hole in it,
                 1 without a hole
                 String or rope to outline a pretend boat

Words that are written in **bold** are when you, the parent, are speaking. Feel free to use your own words.

A Big Idea

Have you ever been fishing? Did you ever go fishing and not catch a single fish? Have you gone fishing and caught lots of fish? How does it feel to not catch any fish? How does it feel to catch lots of fish?

Tell the story of Peter the fisherman in your own words. **When is the best time to catch fish, during the day or at night?** The best fishing is at night. **Peter was a professional fisherman. That means he made his living by catching and selling fish. One day Jesus came to Peter and said, "Let's go fishing." Peter said, "Master, I've been fishing all night and didn't catch anything. But if you want to go, let's go." So Peter and Jesus go fishing during the day, the worst time to fish, and they catch so many fish the boat almost sinks!**

Another time, Jesus went fishing with his disciples. The disciples had been fishing unsuccessfully all night. Jesus told them to put the net on the other side of the boat and they caught so many fish that the boat almost sank.

B Activity

Act out one or both of these stories. Use the rope to outline a boat on the floor (you can also use a couch as the boat). First, the children try fishing on their own and do not catch anything. They act discouraged and tired. Then the person playing Jesus tells them to try fishing again and this time they fill their nets with fish. They are excited and it takes all their strength to get the fish into the boat.

Give the balloon with the hole in it to one of the children. **Blow up this balloon for me.** Child will not be able to do it. **Keep trying. Just blow**

harder. The child may become frustrated. Give child the balloon without the hole and let him try again, this time successfully. (Younger children may not be able to inflate the balloon and will need a parent to help.) **The balloon with the hole represents us when we try to do things on our own. The balloon without the hole represents when we let Jesus help us. Sometimes trying to do things on our own is like running in place or treading water, we're working hard but going nowhere, like blowing and blowing into a balloon with a hole. We waste our energy and become frustrated and discouraged.**

But, when we have Jesus working with us it's like blowing into the other balloon. Jesus can take our efforts and make them grow and grow just like this balloon.

 Application

Read Philippians 4:13. **What do you think this means?** Things that seem too hard for us become easier when Jesus is with us. **Jesus wants to help us.**

Lesson 18:
THE EARLY CHURCH

 TEACHING GOAL: The first Christians had to worship in secret. (This lesson works well for the Monday after Easter or for the Fourth of July.)

1. Play theme song
2. Pray
3. Review last lesson
4. Lesson and discussion
5. Memorize: **We're able to praise Jesus freely today; but only in secret could the early church pray.**
6. Close in prayer

 SCRIPTURE: Acts 8:1-3 "On that day a great persecution broke out against the church at Jerusalem, and all except the apostles were scattered throughout Judea and Samaria. Godly men buried Stephen and mourned deeply for him. But Saul began to destroy the church. Going from house to house, he dragged off men and women and put them in prison."

 MATERIALS: Flashlight

Words that are written in **bold** are when you, the parent, are speaking. Feel free to use your own words.

▲ Big Idea

After Jesus died, was resurrected, and ascended in the clouds to heaven, Christians were persecuted. Do you know what it means to be persecuted? It means that the government can put you in jail or even kill you just

because of what you believe. The Roman government and the Jewish religious leaders persecuted people who said they believed Jesus was the Son of God.

Today, in America, Christians are free to worship Jesus. We don't get in trouble because of what we believe. But do you know that there are still places in the world where people can be put in jail if they say they believe in Jesus?

 **Activity**

After Jesus went to heaven, the early church (the first Christians) had to meet in secret so that they wouldn't get into trouble for believing in Jesus. If you have a crawl space, this is an excellent place to go for the rest of this activity. If you do not have one, a very dark room (a bathroom without windows) will also work. Very quietly lead the family down into the crawl space or into the darkened room and turn on a flashlight.

The early church would meet in secret to sing songs and tell stories about Jesus, his life, and his miracles. Let's sing songs together and tell stories we know about Jesus. Sing songs the children know; let them make requests or tell stories they know.

The early Christians had to hide to keep the soldiers and religious leaders from finding them. I'll bet they had to be very quiet sometimes. Sing in whispers and tell stories in whispers to pretend to be the early church.

 **Application**

If our Bibles were all taken away, we'd still be able to live by the verses we've memorized and by the stories we remember. Most importantly, we allow God to write his words on our hearts. Every day we want to live lives that honor God.

Many people today don't love God and don't follow him. Sometimes they make fun of Christians or laugh at us because we go to church. That doesn't bother us because we love God.

Lesson 19:
BIRTHDAY CAKE FOR JESUS

 TEACHING GOAL: On Christmas we celebrate Jesus' birthday.

1. Play theme song
2. Pray
3. Review last lesson
4. Lesson and discussion
5. Memorize: **On Christmas Day we celebrate; by eating Jesus' birthday cake.**
6. Close in prayer

 SCRIPTURE: Luke 2:11 "Today in the town of David a Savior has been born to you; he is Christ the Lord."

 MATERIALS: Undecorated cake and assorted colors of icings
Candles
Nativity set

 IN ADVANCE: Bake or buy a cake and cover it with a thin layer of white icing. Draw a picture to be copied onto the cake, such as a star or a manger (the kids enjoy helping).

Words that are written in **bold** are when you, the parent, are speaking. Feel free to use your own words.

Big Idea

Tell the Christmas story using the nativity set, emphasizing that Christmas is Jesus' birthday. Compare the balloons, presents, and cakes that kids have at their parties to the lights, trees, and decorations used for Jesus' birthday celebrations today.

Activity

Decorate Jesus' birthday cake. With younger children, the parent may want to outline the picture onto the cake, and then hold the child's hand while he or she fills in the outline with other colors. Write "Happy Birthday Jesus" on the cake.

Light candles and sing, "Happy Birthday" to Jesus. Eat the birthday cake.

 Application

The real meaning of Christmas is about the gift of Jesus Christ. Although many kids can answer that question, the dominant theme of materialism often crowds out the truth. Look for many ways this Christmas to remind yourself and your children about the true meaning of Christmas. It's a great season that provides many opportunities to teach spiritual truths to children.

Lesson 20:
TRAVELING NATIVITY

 TEACHING GOAL: We can celebrate Christmas by acting out the story of Jesus' birth.

1. Play theme song
2. Pray
3. Review last lesson
4. Lesson and discussion
5. Memorize: **Kings, shepherds, and angels came to see the baby Jesus born to Joseph and Mary.**
6. Close in prayer

SCRIPTURE: Luke 2 and **Matthew 2**

MATERIALS: OPTION 1 Pre-made unbreakable nativity set
OPTION 2 Make your own set and characters:
10 Styrofoam cones
10 Styrofoam balls
Water color, washable paint
Toothpicks
Box
Construction paper and markers
Popsicle sticks
Glue
Cotton balls
Hay, straw, or dried grass
Toilet paper rolls
Small piece of cloth
String or thread

Words that are written in **bold** are when you, the parent, are speaking. Feel free to use your own words.

 Big Idea

Read the story of Jesus' birth from a children's Bible or regular Bible.

Talk about the different characters and where they came from to see baby Jesus. Talk about who came to the stable first, second, third, fourth, etc.

B Activity

OPTION 1: Have the children pick different rooms in the house (or areas in a room) to represent the different character locations: (Nazareth, the fields, the East, heaven, Bethlehem). Make signs to place over the doorways to identify the different locations.

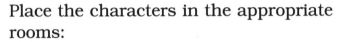

Place the characters in the appropriate rooms:

Mary and Joseph in Nazareth
Shepherds in the fields
Wise men in the East
Angels in heaven
Stable, manger, and sheep
in Bethlehem

Start a few weeks or days before Christmas and move the characters around the house. As it gets closer to Christmas, have the characters move closer to Bethlehem. Mary and Joseph arrive the day before Christmas.

Baby Jesus is in the manger on Christmas morning.

The Shepherds arrive the day after Christmas, and the wise men arrive days or weeks later. Another option is to save a gift from Christmas that the kids can open when the wise men arrive with their gifts for Jesus (possibly on New Year's day).

OPTION 2: Build the nativity set. This activity may involve several weeks of Family Time. Paint the cones and balls using washable paints. Pick colors to define the characters. Color will be the primary way kids tell the characters apart. Following is one option for color combinations:

10 balls (heads): yellow
Mary cone: red

Joseph cone: blue
2 Shepherd cones: orange
3 Wise men cones: purple and pink
3 Angel cones: yellow

After the paint dries, attach the ball heads to the cone bodies with toothpicks and glue.

Make the stable. Cut the top out of a box. The box needs to be big enough to hold the characters. Turn the box on its side with the opening facing forward. This will serve as the stable. You may choose to paint the box or cover it with wood grain contact paper.

Cut the shapes of sheep and/or cows out of construction paper. Glue cotton balls on the sheep. Glue a toilet paper tube on the back of the animals to help them stand.

Make a manger using popsicle sticks and glue. Fill the manger with hay, straw, or dry grass.

Make a star to hang above the stable out of construction paper.

Make a baby Jesus using half of a popsicle stick. Draw a face on the rounded end, and wrap the small piece of cloth around the stick and tie with string or thread.

Continue with the instructions from Option 1.

 **Application**

Part of the significance of the Christmas story is the humble beginning in Bethlehem. Many kids today imagine that Bethlehem had lights, presents, and tremendous fanfare. Although the wise men were likely wealthy, the rest of the story illustrates a poor town, simple shepherds, and ordinary people involved in the story. God wants us to realize that he has come to care for all of us no matter how much money we have or what our social status is. That is the true meaning of Christmas.

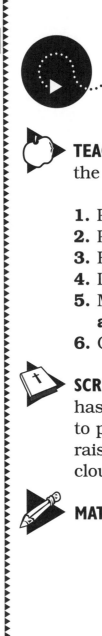

Lesson 21:
EASTER: STORY EGGS

TEACHING GOAL: Twelve symbols can help us remember the story of Easter.

1. Play theme song
2. Pray
3. Review last lesson
4. Lesson and discussion
5. Memorize: **Easter reminds me that Jesus died and rose to set me free.**
6. Close in prayer

SCRIPTURE: Luke 19-24 Jesus enters Jerusalem. Jesus has dinner with his disciples. He goes to Gethsemane to pray. Jesus is arrested. He is crucified, buried, and raised from the dead. He ascends into heaven in the clouds.

MATERIALS: Twelve large, hollow plastic Easter eggs that open
A large piece of paper with twelve 3″ squares making a cross shape
Brown paper or felt
Twigs
12″ string
3 cotton balls
Yellow and brown pipe cleaners
3 nails
White cloth or paper towel strips
5 toothpicks
Rock
4 coins
Bread, grape, or raisin
A picture of Jesus praying or some praying hands
Leaves or construction paper leaves for palm branches

IN ADVANCE: THE TWELVE EGGS AND SYMBOLS
Put the following symbols in 12 eggs and number each
egg.

1. **TRIUMPHAL ENTRY**
   SYMBOL: Palm branches. Use leaves or cut-out
   leaves from construction paper and color them
   green.

2. **MONEY-CHANGERS**
   SYMBOL: Four coins.

3. **LAST SUPPER**
   SYMBOL: Bread, grape, or raisin.

4. **JESUS PRAYING IN THE GARDEN**
   SYMBOL: Find a picture of Jesus praying or draw a
   pair of praying hands.

5. **THE TRIAL**
   SYMBOL: Crown of thorns. Use a small twig or pipe
   cleaner to make the crown.

6. **JESUS CARRIES THE CROSS**
   SYMBOL: A cross. Use jewelry in the shape of a
   cross or make a cross using sticks or toothpicks
   and string.

7. **JESUS DIES FOR OUR SINS**
   SYMBOL: Nails.

8. **JESUS PLACED IN A TOMB**
   SYMBOL: Linens. Thin strips of white cloth or white
   paper towels.

9. **JESUS IS RISEN**
   SYMBOL: Rock.

10. **ANGEL TELLS MARY THAT JESUS IS RISEN**
    SYMBOL: Picture of an angel or yellow pipe cleaner
    in the shape of a halo.

11. **ROAD TO EMMAUS**
    SYMBOL: Cut a piece of brown paper or felt to look
    like a path.

12. **ASCENDING INTO THE CLOUDS**
    SYMBOL: Cotton balls.

Words that are written in **bold** are when you, the parent,
are speaking. Feel free to use your own words.

A Big Idea

At Easter time, we celebrate two events. One, we celebrate the coming of spring, symbolized by egg hunts and bunny rabbits. Two, and most importantly, we celebrate the true Easter story, that is the death and resurrection of Jesus.

In this Family Time we are going to combine both celebrations. We are going to have an Easter egg hunt, and inside the eggs will be symbols to help us tell the Easter story.

B Activity

Hide the numbered eggs for the egg hunt. The kids hunt for the eggs until all twelve are found. Open the eggs one at a time starting with #1 and ending with #12. Tell that part of the Easter Story as you open each egg.

The Easter Story (Matthew, Mark, Luke, and John): **The disciples brought Jesus a donkey to ride into the city of Jerusalem. They put their coats on the donkey to soften the ride. As Jesus rode into Jerusalem, people put coats and (1) palm branches on the road. They shouted, "Hosanna."**

Inside the city walls, Jesus went to the temple and turned over the tables of the money-changers. (2) Money fell all over the ground. Jesus was mad that the merchants were overcharging people. The night before he was arrested, Jesus had a big supper with his friends.

(3) Jesus took bread and wine, gave it to his friends, and said, "Whenever you eat this bread and drink this wine, remember me." That night, Jesus went to the Garden of Gethsemane to (4) pray. While Jesus and his disciples were praying, the Roman soldiers came and arrested Jesus. Jesus was given a quick trial. He was whipped and they put a (5) crown of thorns on his head. Jesus needed help from a man named Simon to carry his (6) cross to a hill called Golgotha or Calvary. Jesus was (7) nailed to the cross and died as an innocent man to pay the price for our sins. Jesus' body was (8) wrapped in linens and placed in a tomb. Three days later when Mary came to the tomb, the (9) rock was rolled away and Jesus was gone! An (10) angel told Mary that Jesus is risen! Later, on the (11) road to a town called Emmaus, Jesus appeared to two disciples. After talking with all the disciples, Jesus said, "Go into all the world and preach the good news to all creation." (Mark 16:15) **Then he ascended into the (12) clouds and now he sits in heaven at the right hand of the throne of God.**

Repeat the egg hunt and have the kids tell the story using the symbols.

▶ Application

The story of the crucifixion and resurrection has a number of important details. This egg hunt and subsequent story give an important overview. Take time over the next few days to elaborate on the details. Several of these eggs each represent mini stories that children will enjoy.

Furthermore, the application of the stories provides the basis for trust, gratefulness to God, and confidence to tell others about Jesus. Be sure to take time and pray to thank God for his remarkable gift of salvation.

Lesson 22:
HALLOWEEN: PUMPKIN PARABLE

TEACHING GOAL: When Jesus comes into our lives, he cleans out the sin so that his light can shine from us.

1. Play theme song
2. Pray
3. Review last lesson
4. Lesson and discussion
5. Memorize: **Jesus takes away our sin; live so others can see him.**
6. Close in prayer

SCRIPTURE: Romans 3:23 "For all have sinned and fall short of the glory of God."

Revelation 3:20 "Here I am! I stand at the door and knock. If anyone hears my voice and opens the door, I will come in."

John 1:29 "The next day John saw Jesus coming toward him and said, 'Look, the Lamb of God, who takes away the sin of the world!'"

Philippians 2:12-13 "Continue to work out your salvation with fear and trembling, for it is God who works in you to will and to act according to his good purpose."

Matthew 5:16 "In the same way, let your light shine before men, that they may see your good deeds and praise your Father in heaven."

2 Corinthians 4:6 "For God, who said, 'Let light shine out of darkness,' made his light shine in our hearts to give us the light of the knowledge of the glory of God in the face of Christ."

John 5:35 "John was a lamp that burned and gave light, and you chose for a time to enjoy his light."

MATERIALS: Pumpkins, carving tools, large spoon
Paper, tape, and markers
Candle

Words that are written in **bold** are when you, the parent, are speaking. Feel free to use your own words.

A Big Idea

(Tell this story while holding and carving a pumpkin.)
In the Bible, God tells us that every person except one has sinned. We have all done things to make Jesus sad, such as saying bad words, hitting others, or disobeying. Every mommy, daddy, son, daughter, brother, sister, grandma, and grandpa has sinned; everyone you know has sinned.

Jesus is the only one without sin. No lies, no hating others, no punching, no whining, no bad words. The Bible says that when we welcome Jesus into our hearts, he will forgive us and help us not to sin as much!

B Activity

Cut the top out of the pumpkin and let the kids see inside. **What is inside the pumpkin?** Seeds, pulp, sticky stuff. **How does the stuff feel inside?** Let each person feel the pumpkin's insides. Yucky, icky.

The pumpkin represents you or me. The hole we cut in the top represents our heart being open. In the Bible Jesus says that he stands at the door of our hearts and knocks. If we hear his knock,

and open the door, then he will come in. My hand
is Jesus coming into our hearts to clean out the sin.
The seeds and pulp are the sin that Jesus removes.

Tell the rest of the story while you work together to clean out
the pumpkin. **When we believe in Jesus and commit our
lives to him, then he comes into our hearts and starts to
take out the yucky stuff in our lives—just like we are
taking the yucky stuff out of this pumpkin. When the sin
has been removed from our lives, then others will begin
to see Jesus in the way we live.**

 Application

**To take the yucky stuff out of our lives, Jesus had to die
on the cross. He was crucified to take away our sins—
yucky stuff—but remember, three days later he came
back to life.** Cut a cross into the pumpkin. You can add slits
to represent rays coming from the center of the cross that
will allow more light to shine through. **When Jesus takes
away our sins and lives in our hearts, then others will see
Jesus in us.** Place a candle in the pumpkin and light it. **The
candle represents Jesus inside our hearts and shining out
for others to see. Let's live so that others will see the
light of Jesus in the things we do, the things we say,
and the way we treat each other.**

TIPS: It's recommended to have one adult per younger child.
The adult needs to control the use of the carving knives.

Lesson 23:
PRAYER WALL

 TEACHING GOAL: God wants us to pray about everything.

1. Play theme song
2. Pray
3. Review last lesson
4. Lesson and discussion
5. Memorize: **God knows what's best; for our prayers and requests.**
6. Close in prayer

SCRIPTURE: Ephesians 6:18 "And pray in the Spirit on all occasions with all kinds of prayers and requests. With this in mind, be alert and always keep on praying."

Ephesians 2:20 "Christ Jesus himself as the chief cornerstone."

 MATERIALS: 3″ x 5″ index cards
Crayons or markers
Tape
Magazines with pictures

Words that are written in **bold** are when you, the parent, are speaking. Feel free to use your own words.

 # Big Idea

What is a cornerstone? Listen to answers. **A cornerstone is usually at the corner of two intersecting walls near the front of a building. Sometimes the date when the building was built will be engraved in the cornerstone. Why is the cornerstone important?** Listen to answers. **The cornerstone is indispensable and fundamental to the building.**

Several times in the Bible, Jesus is called the "cornerstone" of the faith. How is Jesus like a cornerstone?

Listen to answers. **The life of a Christian is built on Jesus. Jesus is the most important part of the Christian faith. Without Jesus we would fall down.**

B Activity

We are going to build a special wall and "Jesus" is going to be the cornerstone of this wall. We are going to build a Prayer Wall. It says in Ephesians 6:18 that we are to pray about everything. Read Ephesians 6:18. **These 3 x 5 cards are going to be the bricks in our wall so let's create our own family Prayer Wall.**

- Using the crayons, color the edges of the card or "brick," leaving plenty of blank space on the card for pictures, drawings, and words representing prayer topics.
- Cut out pictures from magazines of things that remind us of what to pray for.
- Make a special brick with the name "Jesus" to serve as the cornerstone at the bottom of the prayer wall.
- Have each family member make several prayer bricks that highlight a specific person, need, or prayer request.
- Using the tape, build a Prayer Wall someplace in your home where family members will see it.

NOTE: Be sure to use tape that will not take paint (or wallpaper) off of walls.

SAMPLE ITEMS TO PUT ON YOUR PRAYER BRICKS

A Missionary	Name of Government Official
Name of Sick Person	Special Need
Character Quality	Christ-like Behavior
Praise Word	Church
Pray for the President	Friend

NOTE: Even though your child may not yet be able to read, some words can be used as long as you tell children what they represent.

 Application

Let's spend a few moments praying. We can ask God for some things like safety and guidance for some of our bricks. Others we want to thank God for. Let's go around the family and each person can pray for one brick on our wall.

Lesson 24:
OVERFLOW OF THE HEART

TEACHING GOAL: The things we see and hear affect how we live life.

1. Play theme song
2. Pray
3. Review last lesson
4. Lesson and discussion
5. Memorize: **What goes in my eye and ear; is what my friends will see and hear.**
6. Close in prayer

SCRIPTURE: Matthew 6:22-23 "The eye is the lamp of the body. If your eyes are good, your whole body will be full of light. But if your eyes are bad, your whole body will be full of darkness. If then the light within you is darkness, how great is that darkness!"

Matthew 12:34-35 "For out of the overflow of the heart the mouth speaks. The good man brings good things out of the good stored up in him."

MATERIALS: Two dinner plates and two short clear glasses
2 Tbsp baking soda per glass
1/2 cup vinegar per glass
Paper and red markers or colored pencils
Two shades of food coloring
Scissors

IN ADVANCE: Draw a picture of a body with a large heart. The body should be big enough for all of the children to see, but without a mouth, eyes, or nose. Place two tablespoons of baking soda in each glass and set aside.

Words that are written in **bold** are when you, the parent, are speaking. Feel free to use your own words.

 **Big Idea**

Give each child two pieces of paper. Draw a heart on each piece of paper and cut them out, or allow the children to draw their own hearts and cut them out. Ask each child to say the name of a good friend. Write the friends' names on the hearts. Tell them the hearts will be used later. **Why do people use hearts on valentines?** It means, "I love you."

We talk about our feelings being inside our bodies and in our hearts. Some people say, "I love you from the bottom of my heart." Or, "Don't hold in your feelings." How do we get feelings inside our hearts? Read Matthew 6:22-23. Then, on the body you created in advance, draw the eyes and ears using markers or colored pencils. Draw arrows going from the eyes and ears down to the heart. Then give some examples of things we see and hear that we store in our heart.

Input	Good	Bad
Videos	Jesus videos	Fighting videos
TV shows	PBS kids' shows	Shows with disrespect
Friends	Being kind	Being unkind
Family	Obey parents	Being sneaky
Music	Bible songs	Songs with bad words

As the children make suggestions of good things that they see and hear, let them help color in the heart until the whole heart is colored red.

Read Matthew 12:34-35. **That means that what is in our heart will come out of our mouth.** Draw in the mouth, and draw arrows from the heart to the mouth. Then draw the arrows coming out of the mouth.

Activity

Place the hearts with the friends' names on the two dinner plates, while reminding the children that these hearts represent their friends' hearts. Place a clear glass containing baking soda on each plate on top of the hearts. Ask the children again for ideas of good things they can see and hear that will go down into their hearts. For each answer, put a drop of food coloring in the first glass. Repeat using a different color in the second glass, putting in a drop for each idea of something bad that they can see or hear that goes into their hearts.

IN ONE QUICK POUR, add the vinegar to each glass. The colored mixture will bubble up and spill over the glass onto the heart.

Application

Show how the color representing good things spills onto the hearts of their friends and how the color representing bad things spills onto the hearts of their friends. **What we say and do goes into the eyes and ears of our friends and into their hearts.**

Jesus wants us to see and hear good things so that only good will flow out of us and into others.

Lesson 25:
THE THRONE

 TEACHING GOAL: When we live with God on the throne we make choices that are pleasing to him.

1. Play theme song
2. Pray
3. Review last lesson
4. Lesson and discussion
5. Memorize: **God alone; sits on the throne.**
6. Close in prayer

SCRIPTURE: Revelation 12:7-9 "And there was war in heaven. Michael and his angels fought against the dragon, and the dragon and his angels fought back. But he was not strong enough, and they lost their place in heaven. The great dragon was hurled down—that ancient serpent called the devil, or Satan, who leads the whole world astray. He was hurled to the earth, and his angels with him."

Genesis 3:1-5 "Now the serpent was more crafty than any of the wild animals the LORD God had made. He said to the woman, 'Did God really say, "You must not eat from any tree in the garden"?' The woman said to the serpent, 'We may eat fruit from the trees in the garden, but God did say, "You must not eat fruit from the tree that is in the middle of the garden, and you must not touch it, or you will die."' 'You will not surely die,' the serpent said to the woman. 'For God knows that when you eat of it your eyes will be opened, and you will be like God, knowing good and evil.'"

Exodus 32:1-10 "When the people saw that Moses was so long in coming down from the mountain, they gathered around Aaron and said, 'Come, make us gods who will go before us.'... He took what they handed him and made it into an idol cast in the shape of a calf.... 'These are your gods, O Israel, who brought you up out of Egypt.'... 'I have seen these people,' the LORD said.... 'Now leave me alone so that my anger may burn against them and that I may destroy them.'"

Psalm 11:4 "The LORD is in his holy temple; the LORD is on his heavenly throne. He observes the sons of men; his eyes examine them."

Revelation 3:21 "'To him who overcomes, I will give the right to sit with me on my throne, just as I overcame and sat down with my Father on his throne.'"

MATERIALS: Play dough (recipe included)
Chairs—one for every participant
Music

IN ADVANCE: Make play dough (make enough for each child):

1/2 cup salt	1 c flour	1 c water
1 T oil	1 t cream of tartar	
Food coloring		

Mix together ingredients in a saucepan. Cook on medium heat, stirring constantly until mixture pulls away from the sides of the pan. Knead until cool. Put the prepared play dough in plastic bags, one bag for each child.

This lesson is best done with another family or two. In advance tell others about your Family Time experience and invite them to join in with you for an evening. Not only will your friends enjoy having Family Time, but they may catch a vision for having their own regular Family Times too.

Words that are written in **bold** are when you, the parent, are speaking. Feel free to use your own words.

 **Big Idea**

Where does a king sit? On a throne. **Have you ever seen a throne? How is a throne different from a regular chair? Why does a king sit on a throne?**

A throne has come to symbolize the place where the most important person sits. And the person who sits on the throne is the one who makes the final decisions about what to do.

What do you think it means when someone asks, "Who sits on the throne of your life?" Allow time for answers or guesses. **It means, who is king of your life? Who is the most important person in your life and who makes the decisions on what you do?**

For Christians, God is the most important part of our lives. God makes the decisions that are best for us. In several places the Bible describes God as sitting on a throne. When God is on the throne of our lives and we respect him as the most important person in our lives and we follow his decisions, then life is good. The trouble starts when we consider ourselves or something else more important than God and when we think we know better than God.

 **Activity**

(If you have older and younger children, have the older children make the play dough, with supervision, and then help the younger children make their animals and thrones. Older children may still enjoy making sculptures out of the dough!) Give each child some play dough and ask them to make a throne and an animal. Have them describe their throne and animal. Have them place the thrones and animals out of reach but in sight.

There are several stories in the Bible about people who thought they should be on the throne instead of God. In other words, they thought they could make better decisions than God.

Satan thought he should be on the throne instead of God. He got other angels to join him, and they fought God in heaven for control. God won and kicked Satan and his followers out of heaven.

Adam and Eve thought they should be on the throne, that they could make better decisions than God. God told them not to eat the fruit, but they ate it anyway because they wanted to know good and evil like God.

The Israelites thought they should be on the throne. They wanted a God they could see, so when Moses went to climb the mountain, they melted their jewelry and made their own god in the shape of a calf. They started worshipping a calf that they made!

Bring back the play dough animals and place them in front of each child. **Do you think this animal that you made has any special powers? Can it make you smarter or make you stronger? Can it make you feel better when you're sick? What would happen if you prayed to this play dough animal?**

It seems kind of silly to think any of this would happen, but did you know that you and I do the same kind of silly things? We think we know what is best and make silly decisions that get us into trouble, when we should listen to God and follow his decisions.

Let's smash our play dough animals into a ball and put them back into the plastic bags.

Let's play musical throne. You will need one family member to start and stop the music. One chair for each family member playing the Musical Throne game. This is like musical chairs except instead of having one less chair you designate one chair to be the throne. Select one chair to be the throne. Put the chairs and throne in a circle. **Help me decorate this chair with a blanket and jewelry so that it looks special. This is the throne. When the music starts, everyone moves in a clockwise circle around the chairs. When the music stops, find a chair. No one can sit in the throne except Jesus so if you do not have a chair you are out of the game.** Take a chair out of the game and repeat.

This game teaches us that only Jesus is the one who should sit on the throne. Jesus is the one who needs to make the decisions in our lives.

 ## Application

Let's make a list of times when we think we can make better decisions than God. In other words, times when we want to sit on the throne instead of recognizing that God is the king on the throne. Can anyone think of times when we think we know better than God? (Examples may vary.)

1. **God tells us in his Word that children are to obey their parents. Can you think of times when children disobey their parents because they think they know better than parents?**

2. **God tells us to love one another and to be kind. Can you think of a time when you were playing with your friends and they treated someone unkindly?**

3. **God wants us to spend time with him. He tells us in the Bible to pray, to think about good things, to sing songs of praise, and to learn the Bible. When I get to the end of the day and I've spent four hours playing video games and watching TV, but haven't prayed, worshipped God, or learned about the Bible, am I not saying "I know better than God how to use my time"?**

Whenever we try to take God off the throne in our lives, that is to make decisions different from God's decisions, there are consequences. Bad things happen.

On a piece of paper make two columns. Label the first column "Our Decisions" and the second column "Consequences." List the examples used so far and talk about the consequences.

OUR DECISIONS	CONSEQUENCES
Satan's battle against God	Kicked out of heaven. Will live forever apart from God.
Adam and Eve ate the fruit	Kicked out of the garden. Living became hard work. Sin and separation from God.
Israelites and the calf	God was angry. Moses ground up the calf and made them drink it. 3,000 were killed. A plague came on everyone.
Disobeying parents	You may get hurt or sick. Your relationship with your parents is strained. You miss out on blessings.
Being unkind to friends	People get hurt. You get used to being unkind and become a person others don't want to be around. Friendships are damaged.
Not spending time with God	Relationship with God feels impersonal, like God is not there. We get used to living without God and make bad decisions that lead to more trouble.

Index

Seeing is Believing (ALL AGES)

Playing for Keeps (ALL AGES)

Running the Race (ALL AGES)

Wiggles, Giggles, & Popcorn (PRESCHOOLERS)

Index

Bubbles, Balloons, & Chocolate (PRESCHOOLERS)

Tried and True (TEENS)

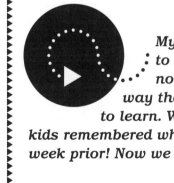
95

You Will Benefit from
OTHER RESOURCES
for YOUR FAMILY

Discover practical, biblical tools to help you build strong bonds in your relationships at home. Find parenting books, CDs, and DVDs to help you parent from a heart-based perspective. Children's curriculum is available to teach your child the same concepts you are learning. **Free Email Parenting Tips** encourage you on a weekly basis. **Learn more at www.biblicalparenting.org.**

Free EMAIL PARENTING Tips

Receive practical, biblical parenting advice a couple times a week in your inbox. Sign up online at www.biblicalparenting.org. Also available in Spanish. Visit www.padresefectivos.org.

Sign up for Free Email Parenting Tips now. (You can remove yourself from the list at any time.) Your email address will not be shared or sold to others.

To learn more give us a call or visit biblicalparenting.org

NATIONAL CENTER for BIBLICAL Parenting

76 Hopatcong Drive
Lawrenceville, NJ 08648-4136
Phone: (800) 771-8334
Email: parent@biblicalparenting.org